CELESTIALS

poems by

Robert Lima

Finishing Line Press
Georgetown, Kentucky

CELESTIALS

Copyright © 2017 by Robert Lima
ISBN 978-1-63534-111-9 First Edition
All rights reserved under International and Pan-American Copyright Conventions. No part of this book may be reproduced in any manner whatsoever without written permission from the publisher, except in the case of brief quotations embodied in critical articles and reviews.

ACKNOWLEDGMENTS

Some of the poems in this collection were written under a Cintas Fellowship in Poetry.
"Astrals" won the first Phi Kappa Phi poetry competition and appeared in the international honor society's journa*l PKP Forum* in April 2009.
"Azimuth," and "Angularity" appeared in *Ometeca: Science and Literature*, Spring 1989.
"Moon Dip" appeared in *The Centre Daily Times*, July 20, 2009.

Publisher: Leah Maines

Editor: Christen Kincaid

Cover Art: NASA, public domain

Author Photo: Mark X. Lima

Cover Design: Elizabeth Maines

Printed in the USA on acid-free paper.
Order online: www.finishinglinepress.com
       also available on amazon.com

> Author inquiries and mail orders:
> Finishing Line Press
> P. O. Box 1626
> Georgetown, Kentucky 40324
> U. S. A.

Table of Contents

Airview	1
Angel	2
Angularity	3
Apollo Rushing	4
Astrals	5
Azimuth	6
Cloud Cover	7
Comet	8
Debacle	9
Descent	10
Diorama	11
East	12
Extremities	13
Fallen Stars	14
Golden Isles	15
Map	16
Moon	17
Moon Dip	18
Mythos	19
Naked Singularities	20
Night Flight	21
Seeing White	22
Setting Sun	23
Solstice	24
Southwest	25
Stars	26
Sun at Noon	27
Sweat of the Sun	28
Tears of the Moon	28
Vacancy	29
West	30

AIR VIEW

The darkling shadows

ephemeral clouds design.

Passive earth below.

ANGEL

See him as they did
in some long ago:
Shining white
halo round his head
wings upon his back
easing through
the firmament

Bright new angel of light
poised against the dark
without tether
to the ship in orbit
illuminating life

ANGULARITY

First meeting in space.

Melding patterns of our
angularity
changing into curvilinear
touches
of points and sides
resolving towards
rhythmic swells of
interpenetration
in the Time/Space
continuum

APOLLO RUSHING

to barren Moon,
the rape of fertile Venus,
the clash with Mars
are left without a second
in our rhetoric

We are content
to spend ourselves
with reason

Let others put a dream to work

ASTRALS

*"We are such stuff as
dreams are made on."*
Shakespeare

We have been taught our bodies came from dust,
to dust, then, would return at death.

Tonight, I learned that only half a truth was told
for wise astronomers, as one, now state
that stardust was the matrix ore
of which all things were ultimately made
when, primally, a Supernova burst
and sprinkled its debris across
the far-flung galaxy that's our abode.

Since then, our bodies, made of astral dust,
are longing to locate themselves once more
among the womb of stars.

AZIMUTH

Angular degrees or mils
distanced clockwise
from the northern point

Horizon's arc
measured therefrom
to a vertical,

arc passing from the zenith
through the center of a star
as in our juncture

with the Universe

CLOUD COVER

I

Waking from half sleep to light,
I find I fly above the continent of clouds,
a lush terrain of white below,
its glaciers, pinnacles, depressions
like white Antarctic vastness,
light and dark in interplay
of nuance on the bleak cloudscape
between hard edge and full shadow,
nestled against azure
as in the mind's eye at awakening
after taking flight

II

Ephemerals of wispy puffs
glide eerily above the continent of clouds
like gypsies bent on some subversive act

III

The great white tundra in the sky,
furrowed by its inner wind,
becomes a glacial ridge
above the ample thighs of hills

IV

Where do clouds go
when we no longer see
the continent of clouds?

COMET

> hurtling out of spatial sky
> scorching atmospheres
> through which it arcs,
> millennial and consummate
>
> dead body
> seemingly alive with fiery tail
> burning through the night
> into the reverie of hotted flesh

DEBACLE

The Sun
d
e
s
c
e
n
d
s
like gold
wasting
its
substance
to render
v i e w s
through
our
pollution

DESCENT

Leaving the once-bright star
dissolving into barely light,
the sky into the water
limitless and dark

Seeking the depths from heights,
descending beyond tolerance
to the murky level of bottom life

Descending into fathoms,
going down through the fear.

DIORAMA

        Blackness . . .
       points of light
          emerge
            reverberate
                 design

      The interaction
       of our forms
    as on a plane of stars

EAST

Rising,
The orb of gold
Casts
Its rays
Upon the dark
And
Sends the shades
Of night
Scattering
To the darker side

There is a breath
Of wellness
In attendant winds,
The land
Begets the produce
Of its warmth,
While seas
Bask in the touch
Of splendor
That luminescence
Brings

And day begins
A new trajectory
Of light

EXTREMITIES

We have a man in the heights of Space
flying untethered in the void,
cutting arcs above our sphere
through the miracle of self-propulsion.

No umbilical cord for the likes of him;
he's severed all ties to the mother ship,
out of its cargo hold on his own,
seemingly still at incredible speeds.

We have a man spaced out of his heights.

FALLEN STARS

We are
five points
of anatomy...

a pentagram alive
in metamorphosis
striving to regain
our once-held heights
in metaspace

...flailing air
like butterflies

THE GOLDEN ISLES

As old hexameters resound
with solar lust of gods and beasts,
and at the darkening of day,
when long-winged birds depart from marble ruins,
the wind resuscitates among last laurel trees
the calming murmur of Socratic fugues—
philosophy of stellar caste which transmigrated
out of myths and fables told relentlessly
within the span of man in time.

The tracks of the celestial bull
still lie upon the blue sea's edge.
The joyous songs are still becoming
in the shepherds' flutes of night.

MAP

> The Moon
> must never be
> so close
> that we can
> touch it

MOON

              The
         puff of tissue
           overhead
           has been
         crumpled into
          contours &
           divides,
           rounded
          in the palm
           of some
        enchanted night
         and powdered
              for
            delight

MOON DIP

Moon
you were my sadness
pictured in your
solitude

I spoke your name
in syllables
of gold,
of tangerine
of silver tone

That was in reverie
before your fall

MYTHOS

Chimor nobility descended from two stars
whose progeny, the Founder Taycanamo,
came ashore on a long raft, proclaiming:

> "The Great Lord sent me
> from across the Sea
> to govern Men and
> this whole Land."

And from Him came nine other Kings
who built nine palaces which served
as tombs for their remains as well as
those of whomsoever they possessed.

Their Souls ascended to the Sky
replenishing the pantheon of Gods
until the Inka conquered their domain.

NAKED SINGULARITIES
Physical Review Letters
February 25, 1991

If they exist, they shake some underpinnings of
the cosmic theory set by Einstein,
ideas on matter, gravity, as well as
space and time—the relativity of each to each.

Naked singularities may be resultants of
gigantic clouds of particles collapsing on themselves,
their regions near the pointed ends
condensing into areas infinite in density and weight.

There is grave danger in all this for Nature
is believed unable to produce such dire effects,
create a force that has no bounds, is infinite,
and, naked, lies beyond the gravity black holes contain,

themselves perceived to be, but still unproved.
The singularities that may exist therein are clothed,
but yet they are unable to communicate their selves
for nothing in black holes can reach our ken

and anything approaching their serenity would find
its very being wrenched and torn to shreds.
Indeed "There are more things in heaven and earth
than are dreamt of in our philosophy," or Einstein's,

and the dilemma of "To be or not to be" takes on
significance beyond the existential stage of man on Earth
when naked singularities that had no possibility of life
intrude upon the very fabric of the Universe's sense.

NIGHT FLIGHT

We chase the night all night
in flight across pacific sea,
through never ending West where
day dies with the Sun.

We trace the dawning light
in wending through the clouds,
and enter the far East in time
to resurrect the Sun.

SEEING WHITE

Driving East
Through heavy dawning fog,
The sun is white as ice—
Large like a full midnight moon—
And yet, its brightness
Cannot mitigate the fog,
A diaphanous body of white
That casts a shroud around
The early morning road
And on the eyes that strain
Behind the wheel
Seeking sight

SETTING SUN

The Great Cadaver of Gold
absconds with light
into the silver lining
of the casket cloud

SOLSTICE

I
Above the
Southern Hemisphere
the Sun
attains its farthest point
away from Earth
and halts
its north, south progress
on entering Cancer
water sign

II
At thermal springs
the people gather
for the healing
of waters
sacred to the Sun

III
In villages
they light the fires
of exhortation

that Sun be strengthened
that evil be allayed
that grains grow tall
that life's fertility endure

The fire leaping,
Summer's height

SOUTHWEST

The Moon, one night from fullness,
witnessed the cold breath of Winter
riding roughshod in the pocket of Wind
over dark hills trembling without
the overcoat of their deciduous leaves.

Owl hooted.
Coyote bayed.
Bat winged.

Somewhere, Night carried an air
played by Kokopeli on his flute,
his silhouette bent into the dark
in curvature against the Moon,
the song heralding transcendence.

STARS

                         dug
                      into night
                   sand crabs in
                 womb privacy

                 remnant dark
                  at summer's
                     dawn

THE SUN AT NOON

The sun at noon
bleaches bones of whales
and other mammals
upon the beaches of
the southern hemisphere
where they have come
to rest

These bones
may have the same
denouement
while still in life
if they have strayed
and lost tenacity

SWEAT OF THE SUN

Coursing through space
in ecstatic mutation
out of sunflares
it is ingrained
within the entrails
beneath our feet
in veins of gold

*

TEARS OF THE MOON

Droplets
from a dead form
become slivers of
s i l v e r
embedded in earth

VACANCY

> The sky at night
> is a mirage
> reflecting lights
> unreal.
>
> The stars
> have moved beyond
> to hills.

WEST

> Cardinal Point
> of Darkness,
> Seat of Demons,
> abode of Spirits
> of Samhain.
>
> Occident,
> where the Sun
> goes to
> die.

ROBERT LIMA is Professor Emeritus of Spanish and Comparative Literatures, as well as Fellow Emeritus of the Institute for the Arts and Humanistic Studies, at The Pennsylvania State University. In 2003. He was dubbed Knight Commander in the Order of Queen Isabel of Spain by His Majesty King Juan Carlos I.

He is the author of forty books of poetry, criticism, biography, bibliography and translation. Over five hundred of his own poems have appeared worldwide, and well over one hundred-fifty of his professional articles have been published in refereed journals.

A participant in the 1960s New York City poetry scene, he read at Café Cino, Tenth Street Coffeehouse, "Les Deux Megots," and Judson Memorial Church, all in Greenwich Village or the East Village. He founded & co-edited the anthology *Seventh Street. Poems of "Les Deux Megots"* and *Judson Review* (2nd series).

His books of poetry include *Fathoms* (1981), *The Olde Ground* (1985), *Mayaland* (1992), *Sardinia / Sardegna* (2000), *Tracking the Minotaur* (2003), *The Pointing Bone* (2008), *The Rites of Stone* (2010), *Self* (2012), *Por caminos errantes* (2014), and *CELESTIALS* (2017). "The Poetic World of Robert Lima: A Retrospective" was an exhibit at Pattee Library from March through August 2004. His poem "Astrals" won the first Phi Kappa Phi poetry competition and appeared in the society's journal *FORUM*. His readings are recorded on the CDs *Eye of the Beholder* and *Tracking the Minotaur*.

He has been a Cintas Foundation Fellow in Poetry, Senior Fulbright-Hays Fellow, Poet-in Residence at U. of San Marcos in Perú. Commonwealth Speaker of the Pennsylvania Humanities Council, and a member of the Poetry Society of America, PEN, Academician of the Academia Norteamericana de la Lengua Española and Corresponding Member of the Real Academia Española.

He is listed in *Who's Who in the World*, *Who's Who in America*, *World Who's Who of Authors*, and other creative writing directories in the U.S. and abroad.
http://www.personal.psu.edu/RXL2

www.ingramcontent.com/pod-product-compliance
Lightning Source LLC
LaVergne TN
LVHW041511070426
835507LV00012B/1478